NATION OF
IMMIGRANTS

J
SMITH

12 IMMIGRANTS WHO MADE THE
AMERICAN
MILITARY GREAT

by Paige Smith

12 STORY LIBRARY

www.12StoryLibrary.com

12-Story Library is an imprint of Bookstaves.

Photographs ©: Library of Congress, cover, 1; H. B. Hall/US National Archives and Records Administration/PD, 4; Felix Lipov/Shutterstock.com, 5; National Museum of the US Navy/PD, 6; Library of Congress, 7; National Museum of the US Navy/PD, 7; PD, 8; Library of Congress, 8; Library of Congress, 9; DEPARTMENT OF THE NAVY -- NAVAL HISTORICAL CENTER/PD, 10; Robert Knox Sneden/PD, 11; PD, 12; US Coast Guard/PD, 13; Everett Collection Historical/ Alamy Stock Photo, 14; PD, 15; PD, 16; US National Archives and Records Administration/ PD, 17; US Army, 18; Jerome Howard/US Army, 19; RUSSELL ROEDERER/US Army, 20; US Department of Defense, 21; US Army Sgt. First Class Clydell Kinchen/PD, 22; J.D. Leipold/ US Army, 23; Sgt. Elizabeth Thurson/US Marine Corps, 24; Staff Sgt. Greg Thomas/US Department of Defense, 25; MarineCorps NewYork/CC2.0, 26; Minnesota National Guard/ CC2.0, 27; Library of Congress, 28; PD, 29

ISBN
978-1-63235-579-9 (hardcover)
978-1-63235-633-8 (paperback)
978-1-63235-694-9 (ebook)

Library of Congress Control Number: 2018948080

Printed in the United States of America
Mankato, MN
June 2018

About the Cover
John Ericsson in 1865.

Access free, up-to-date content on this topic plus a full digital version of this book. Scan the QR code on page 31 or use your school's login at 12StoryLibrary.com.

Table of Contents

Casimir Pulaski Is the Father of the American Cavalry

Casimir Pulaski was a heroic freedom fighter for two countries. First, he fought in his own country, Poland. Then he fought in the American Revolution.

Pulaski was born on March 6, 1745, in Warsaw, Poland. As a young man, he joined his father to defend their country against Russia. By age 21, he was a commander in the military.

In 1776, Pulaski met American statesman Benjamin Franklin in Paris. He was inspired by America's struggle for independence from England. Pulaski arrived in America in June 1777. He fought next to General George Washington. At the Battle of Brandywine on September 11, he led a successful charge against the British. He is credited with saving Washington's life. Four days later, Washington made Pulaski brigadier general of the American cavalry.

In 1778, Pulaski formed the Pulaski Cavalry Legion. Many of his men were immigrants from Germany, France, Ireland, and Poland. This was the first true cavalry legion in the Continental Army. Pulaski

Statue of Casimir Pulaski at Freedom Plaza in Washington, DC.

became known as the Father of the American Cavalry. In October 1779, at the Battle of Savannah, Pulaski was badly wounded. He died two days later. Pulaski was 34 years old.

In 1929, the US Congress proclaimed October 11 of each year Pulaski Day. In 2009, they made Pulaski an honorary citizen of the United States. Hundreds of towns, counties, monuments, streets, parks, and bridges have been named after him. A Pulaski Day Parade is held each year in New York City.

7
Number of US counties named after Casimir Pulaski.

- Casimir Pulaski came to America in 1777 to fight in the Revolutionary War.
- He is credited with saving George Washington's life.
- Pulaski died in 1779 fighting as an immigrant for America.
- Congress made him an honorary US citizen in 2009.

John Ericsson's Inventions Help the North Win the Civil War

John Ericsson was a Swedish American inventor and engineer. His ideas helped the Union Navy during the US Civil War.

Ericsson was born on July 31, 1803, in Värmland, Sweden. He was good at drawing and solving problems. During his twenties, Ericsson had ideas for improving warships. For example, if the engines could be moved below decks,

under the waterline, they would be safer from enemy fire. But most ships had paddlewheels. This idea wouldn't work with paddlewheels. So Ericsson came up with a new design for a screw propeller.

In 1839, Ericsson immigrated to the United States. He thought the fast-growing country would be interested in his propeller. By 1844, Ericsson's propeller was in use by 25 ships on the Great Lakes. In 1848, Ericsson became a US citizen.

When the Civil War began in 1861, every ship in the Union navy was made of wood. Confederate ships could fire exploding shells. The North looked to Ericsson for help. He designed an ironclad ship. It was built very quickly. The USS *Monitor* had armored plates on the hull. It had no masts or sails. Everything was below the waterline, except one

100
Number of working days it took to build the USS *Monitor*.

- John Ericsson had ideas for improving warships at a young age.
- He immigrated to the United States in 1839.
- He is best known as the designer of the USS *Monitor*.

THE VICTORIOUS UNION GUNBOAT "MONITOR."

Published by Caldwell & Co., 37 Park row.

Officers on the deck of the USS *Monitor*.

special feature. The world's first rotating gun turret was up top.

The Confederacy built its own ironclad, the CSS *Virginia*. On March 9, 1862, the *Monitor* and the *Virginia* met in battle. There was no clear winner, but the battle changed how wars would be fought on water. The time of wooden warships was over.

Ericsson kept inventing until his death in March 1889. Today he is remembered as one of the top inventors of the nineteenth century.

Sarah Emma Edmonds Serves in the Civil War as a Man

Sarah Emma Edmonds was born in New Brunswick, Canada, in 1841. She grew up on her parents' farm. At 15, her father tried to force her into an arranged marriage. Instead, Sarah ran away. She immigrated to the United States. She knew it would be hard to travel alone as a woman and get a job. So she cut her hair and dressed like a man. She changed her name to Franklin Thompson. She settled in Michigan and sold Bibles for a living.

When the US Civil War began, she enlisted in the Union Army. As Franklin Thompson, she worked as a field nurse. When the Army needed spies, she volunteered. The Army didn't keep records of her spy work. But Edmonds later wrote a book called *The Female Spy of the Union*

Sara Edmonds on the left, and as Franklin Thompson on the right.

Army. In the book, she describes disguising herself as a black man named Cuff. Edmonds wore other disguises, too. She completed at least 11 secret missions.

In 1863, Edmonds came down with malaria. To avoid discovery, she went to a private hospital. Before she could return, the Army listed her as a deserter. Edmonds worked as a nurse outside the Army until the end of the war. Later in life, she petitioned the War Department to change her deserter status. Eventually she was granted an honorable discharge.

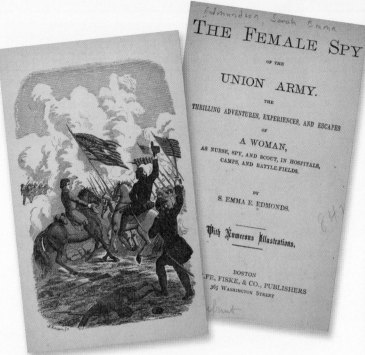

AFTER THE WAR

In 1882, Sarah Emma Edmonds told the War Department that she and Franklin Thompson were the same person. Fellow soldiers spoke on her behalf. In 1884, the US Congress gave her an honorable discharge and a pension. The desertion charge was removed in 1886.

$13
Monthly salary for a Union private in 1863..

- Sarah Emma Edmonds disguised herself as a man and changed her name.
- When the Civil War began, she enlisted in the Union Army as Franklin Thompson.
- She worked as a nurse and a spy.

Philip Bazaar Risks His Life in the Civil War

The USS *Santiago de Cuba* in 1864.

Philip Bazaar was a Chilean American seaman in the Union Navy during the US Civil War. He was one of the first Hispanic Americans to be awarded the Medal of Honor.

Bazaar was born January 1, 1838, in Chile, a country in South America. His family immigrated to Bedford, Massachusetts, in 1863. They were seeking a better life. Phillip loved his newly adopted country. But he soon learned the United States was in conflict.

The North and the South were at war with each other. In May 1864, Bazaar enlisted in the Union Navy.

Seaman Bazaar was assigned to a wooden side-wheeler ship called the USS *Santiago de Cuba*. The ship served off the coast of North Carolina. It was part of a blockade against the Confederacy. In 1865, Union General Ulysses S. Grant attacked Fort Fisher. The fort was a Confederate stronghold. Bazaar volunteered to help carry messages

4

Number of years the US Civil War lasted (1861–1865).

- Bazaar joined the Union Navy in 1864 as a seaman.
- He delivered messages to officers on shore during a heavy attack.
- Bazaar was awarded the Medal of Honor for his bravery.

THINK ABOUT IT

Philip Bazaar joined the Union Navy shortly after arriving to the United States. Would you be willing to defend your new country as an immigrant? What are some rights you would fight for?

to officers on shore. He entered the Confederate fort under heavy assault. He successfully delivered the messages. And he helped his fellow soldiers return to the ship. Bazaar risked his own life. For his bravery, Bazaar was awarded the Medal of Honor. This is the United States' highest personal military decoration.

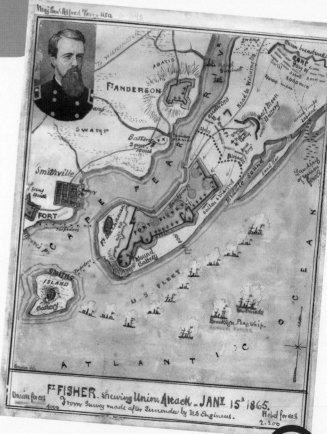

Igor Sikorsky Is the Father of the Helicopter

Igor Sikorsky was a Russian American inventor and aviation engineer. As a boy, he saw a drawing made by the artist Leonardo da Vinci. It was a drawing of a rotary-wing aircraft. Sikorsky dreamed of making one someday.

Sikorsky was born on May 25, 1885, in Kiev. The city was then part of Russia. As a young man, Sikorsky worked on early versions of a helicopter. But he couldn't get them to lift off the ground. He went on to design other aircraft. In 1909, Sikorsky made a biplane that flew for 12 seconds. In 1913, he made the first four-engine airplane. It was used as a bomber in World War I. By then, Sikorsky had his own airplane factory in Kiev.

Sikorsky immigrated to the United States in 1919. Before long, other Russians helped him start a company in the US. Composer Sergei Rachmaninoff invested $5,000 in Sikorsky's company. That amount would be worth about $73,000 today. In 1928, Sikorsky became a US citizen. His company made large aircraft. Pan American bought a fleet.

Sikorsky in his helicopter in 1944.

In 1939, Sikorsky finally made his first working helicopter. It could fly, hover, and maneuver. The US Army Air Corps gave him a contract. In World War II, Sikorsky's helicopters saved many lives. During the Korean War, they proved themselves in battle. Today helicopters are used by military forces all over the world.

115

Miles per hour that Sikorsky's first twin-engine aircraft flew in 1923.

- Igor Sikorsky immigrated to America in 1919.
- A fellow Russian, Sergei Rachmaninoff, invested in Sikorsky's aircraft company.
- Today helicopters are used by the military around the world.

SAYING THANK YOU

Igor Sikorsky was grateful for Sergei Rachmaninoff's support. He named his first son after the composer. Sergei Sikorsky was born in 1925. He followed in his father's footsteps and worked at Sikorsky Aircraft until he retired in 1992.

Hector P. García Fights for Veterans' Rights

Hector P. García was a Mexican American doctor and decorated war veteran. He helped Hispanic veterans receive military benefits after World War II.

García was born in Mexico on January 17, 1914. In 1917, his family fled the Mexican revolution and settled in Texas. García's parents were educators.

They taught their children to value education. In 1936, García graduated with honors from the University of Texas. He earned his medical degree there in 1940. García enlisted in the Army in 1942 to serve in World War II. He was an infantry officer and surgeon. For his service, García was awarded the Bronze Star.

García returned to Texas and started a medical practice. He saw how hard life was for migrant workers and veterans. He got involved in politics and his community. García discovered that Mexican American veterans were being denied military benefits. The GI Bill of 1944 promised benefits to all veterans. These helped with housing, education, and health care. But Mexican Americans weren't getting theirs. To right these wrongs, García founded the American GI Forum. The AGIF pushed for equal treatment.

Receiving the Presidential Medal of Freedom from President Ronald Reagan in 1984.

Soon there were AGIF chapters in 40 cities. Hispanic veterans received the benefits they deserved.

García was recognized for his work. In 1967, he was named ambassador to the United Nations. In 1968, he was appointed to the US Commission on Civil Rights. In 1984, he was awarded the Presidential Medal of Freedom by President Ronald Reagan. This is the nation's highest civilian honor. García was the first Mexican American to receive it.

7
Number of US Presidents Garcia advised on Mexican American relations.

- Hector García immigrated to the United States with his family in 1917.
- He founded the American GI Forum in 1948.
- In 1984, he received the Presidential Medal of Freedom.

Mabel Staupers Widens the Door for Black Nurses

Mabel Staupers was a Caribbean American and a nurse. She worked to remove racial barriers in her profession. She wanted black nurses to have the same opportunities as white nurses.

Staupers was born Mabel Doyle on February 27, 1890, in Barbados, West Indies. In 1903, she immigrated with her family to the United States. They settled in Harlem in New York City. Mabel earned her RN (Registered Nurse) diploma in 1917 at the Freedmen's Hospital School of Nursing. In 1920, she helped start the Booker T. Washington Sanitarium. This was Harlem's first clinic for black patients with tuberculosis. Mabel worked hard for better health care for minorities in the Harlem community. A dental service for schoolchildren was started. So was a clinic for patients who couldn't afford to pay for care. In 1931, Mabel married Fitz C. Staupers.

When the United States became involved in World War II, there was a shortage of nurses in the Army Nurse Corps (ANC). The War Department had strict quotas that limited the number of black nurses. In 1943, only 183 black nurses were commissioned. Staupers campaigned for change. She contacted the surgeon general of the army. She lobbied members of Congress. She asked First Lady Eleanor Roosevelt for help. She started a letter-writing campaign. By 1945, both the Army and the Navy accepted black nurses.

In 1951, the National Association for the Advancement of Colored People (NAACP) gave Staupers the Spingarn Medal. This is the NAACP's highest honor.

600
Number of black nurses serving in World War II by the war's end.

- Mabel Staupers immigrated to the United States with her family in 1903.
- She received her RN diploma in 1917.
- She worked hard for better health care for minorities.
- Her efforts helped to eliminate military quotas for black nurses.

Phyllis Mae Dailey (second from right) became the first black nurse in the US Navy on March 8, 1945.

Alfred Rascon Finally Gets His Medal of Honor

Alfred Rascon was born in 1945 in Chihuahua, Mexico. He was four years old when his family immigrated to America. They settled in California. After graduating high school, Rascon enlisted in the US Army. He became a medic.

This was during the Vietnam War. Rascon was sent to Vietnam. In 1966, his platoon came under heavy fire. Many soldiers, including Rascon, were shot. He kept running through enemy fire to help others. When a grenade landed nearby, he covered the body of an injured sergeant with his own body. The blast blew the helmet off his head. He was so badly wounded people thought he would die.

Rascon spent months recovering in an army hospital. He was honorably discharged and returned home. For his bravery, he was nominated for the Medal of Honor. This is the United States' highest personal military decoration. But because of a mistake in the paperwork, Rascon received a Silver Star.

Rascon became a naturalized US citizen. He returned to active duty and did a second tour in Vietnam. Years went by. Then some of the

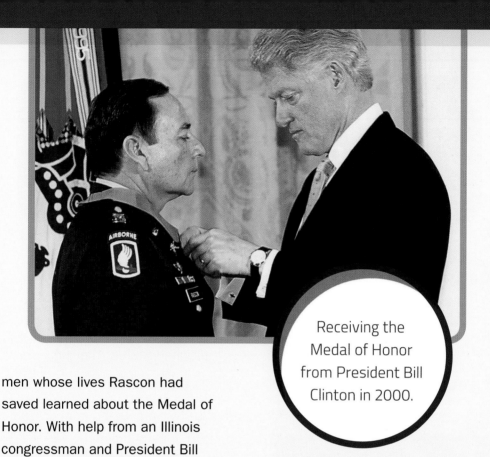

Receiving the Medal of Honor from President Bill Clinton in 2000.

men whose lives Rascon had saved learned about the Medal of Honor. With help from an Illinois congressman and President Bill Clinton, Rascon finally received his overdue Medal of Honor in 2000.

34

Years Alfred Rascon waited to receive his Medal of Honor.

- Alfred Rascon enlisted in the US Army after high school.
- He was nominated for a Medal of Honor after his heroic acts in 1966.
- Rascon received his Medal of Honor in 2000.

THINK ABOUT IT

When Alfred Rascon graduated from high school, he was not yet an American citizen. He couldn't be drafted. So he volunteered for military service, while a war was going on. Why do you think he did that?

John Shalikashvili Becomes America's Top Soldier

John Shalikashvili was 16 years old when he first set foot in the United States. Yet he rose to greatness in the US military.

Born in Warsaw, Poland, in 1936, Shalikashvili grew up during World War II. He and his family lived through the German invasion and occupation of Poland. In 1952, they immigrated to the United States. They became American citizens in 1958.

Shalikashvili graduated from college in 1958. A month later, he was drafted into the US Army. He decided to make the Army his career. He rose quickly through the ranks. Shalikashvili served in Alaska, Germany, and Vietnam. He won the Bronze Star for heroism. He served in Korea, Europe, and the United States. He was noticed by General Colin Powell as someone who got things done.

By 1991, Shalikashvili was known as General Shali. He was put in charge of Operation Provide Comfort. He helped save the lives of countless refugees in northern Iraq. In

29

Number of member countries in NATO.

- John Shalikashvili began his military career as a draftee.
- He led Operation Provide Comfort, which saved many lives.
- He was Chairman of the Joint Chiefs of Staff from 1993 to 1997.

A NOBLE MILITARY FAMILY

General Shali's grandfather was a general in the imperial Russian army. His father was an officer in the Polish army. His older brother, Othar, chose a military career. Othar commanded a parachute infantry regiment in the Vietnam War.

1992, he became Supreme Allied Commander of NATO in Europe. He started NATO's Partnership for Peace program.

In 1993, President Bill Clinton made General Shali Chairman of the Joint Chiefs of Staff. This is a group of senior military leaders who advise the president. Shalikashvili was the first foreign-born soldier to achieve this position. He was also the first draftee. When he retired in 1997, he received the Presidential Medal of Freedom.

Florent Groberg Saves Lives with Selfless Act

Florent "Flo" Groberg was born in Poissy, France, on May 8, 1983. His family immigrated to the United States when he was in middle school. They settled in Maryland. In 2001, Groberg became a naturalized US citizen. After graduating from the University of Maryland, he enlisted in the US Army in 2008.

Groberg served twice in Afghanistan. He spent 2009–2010 in the Kunar Province. In February 2012, he deployed again to Afghanistan. He was promoted to captain in July.

On August 8, 2012, Captain Groberg was escorting 28 American and Afghan military leaders to a security meeting. He noticed a man walking backwards toward them. At first, Groberg wondered if the man was mentally ill. Then the man turned and charged. He was wearing a suicide vest.

Groberg tackled him. The bomb went off. Groberg was thrown into the air. Four people were killed. The explosion made a second bomber's vest blow up prematurely. The blast hit a building. If Groberg hadn't acted

Groberg on helicopter patrol over Kunar Province in July, 2012.

quickly and selflessly, many more people would have been killed.

Somehow Groberg survived. He lost 50 percent of his left calf muscle. He suffered nerve damage, a mild traumatic brain injury, and a blown eardrum. He spent nearly three years recovering at Walter Reed National Military Medical Center. He was medically retired in July 2015.

Groberg's many awards and decoration include the Bronze Star and the Purple Heart. On November 2, 2015, he received the Medal of Honor from President Barack Obama.

20

Number of feet (6 m) Groberg was thrown when the suicide bomber's vest exploded.

- Florent Groberg is a French American immigrant who joined the US Army.
- While serving in Afghanistan, he tackled a suicide bomber.
- His awards include the Medal of Honor.

23

Maria Daume Blazes a Trail in the US Marines

When their mother died, they were sent to an orphanage. Daume remembers drinking juice made from rotten apples. In 2003, the twins were adopted by an American couple.

Growing up in Long Island, New York, Daume was bullied in school. She made herself mentally tough and physically strong. She learned mixed martial arts and jujitsu. When Daume was 12, she went to a fundraiser for people with cancer. Marines were there demonstrating pull-ups and pushups. Daume decided to be a marine someday. She wanted to fight, just like a man. Except the Marine Corps didn't let women fight.

March 23, 2017, was a milestone in the history of the US Marines. That's when a young Private First Class (PFC) graduated from the School of Infantry as a mortarman. Except this mortarman is a woman.

Maria Daume and her twin brother, Nikolai, were born in a Russian prison in 1999.

In December 2015, Ashton Carter, the US Secretary of Defense, made an announcement. All jobs in the military would be open to women. Even combat jobs. In 2016, Daume

went to boot camp. Then she took infantry training. She didn't just complete the training. She crushed it.

Daume hopes other women will follow her example. If you want something, go for it.

220,000

Number of jobs in the military Carter's decision opened to women who qualify.

- Maria Daume spent the first years of her life in a prison and an orphanage.
- She knew when she was 12 that she wanted to be a marine.
- Daume is the first female marine to graduate from infantry training.

A MORTAR MARINE'S TRAINING

As part of her training, Daume had to scale a 56-inch (42-cm) wall in 30 seconds wearing full combat gear. She had to lift an 80-pound (36-kg) machine gun above her head. She had to hike more than 12 miles (19 km) carrying a 60mm mortar system. A mortar is a small cannon.

A Nation of Immigrants in the US Military

Immigrants and other non-citizens have fought for America from the start. People like Casimir Pulaski crossed an ocean to join the Revolutionary War. The Continental Army needed experienced officers. Pulaski was eager to help. In 1776, everyone else in the war, except Native Americans, was an immigrant or descended from immigrants.

In 1860, before the American Civil War began, about 13 percent of the US population was foreign-born. (That's about the same share as today.)

During the war, one in four Union Army soldiers was an immigrant. Most were German or Irish. More than 500,000 immigrants fought for the North. Without them, the North would have lost.

In World War I, about half a million immigrants served in the US military. More than 300,000 immigrants served in World War II. Some 65,000 immigrants are serving today.

Immigrants make the military more diverse. They fill key positions that require special language skills,

cultural knowledge, and medical skills. For immigrants, the military offers jobs and educational opportunities. Service has been a path to US citizenship. Many immigrants who served in the armed forces and met other requirements have become naturalized citizens. From 1907 to 2010, more than 710,000 immigrants were naturalized through military service.

IMMIGRANTS AND THE MEDAL OF HONOR

Created during the American Civil War, the Medal of Honor is the United States' highest personal military decoration. It is awarded for acts of valor, or great courage. It is presented to recipients by the President of the United States in the name of Congress. One in five Medal of Honor recipients is an immigrant.

9.5

Percent of immigrants in the US military who were born in Mexico.

- Immigrants have served in America's military since the birth of the nation.
- Without immigrants, the North would have lost the Civil War.
- Military service has been a path to US citizenship for many immigrants.

More Immigrants in History

LAFAYETTE.

Gilbert du Motier, Marquis de Lafayette

Lafayette was a French aristocrat and military officer. He also fought in the American Revolution. He became a close friend and confidante of George Washington. He secured additional French troops and supplies, and he helped defeat the British. For his actions in France and the US, he is known as the Hero of Two Worlds. He was given honorary US citizenship in 1784.

Baron von Steuben

A German military officer, Baron von Steuben played an important role in the American Revolution. He arrived at Valley Forge in early 1778. This was General George Washington's winter camp. The Continental Army was disorganized and messy. The Baron trained a group of soldiers to march and use the bayonet. He taught them to fire and load their muskets more efficiently. He drilled them in following orders more quickly. Then these soldiers trained other soldiers. The Baron turned the army into a skilled fighting force. He also wrote its first military manual. After the war, he became a US citizen.

Julius Peter Garesché

Lt. Colonel Julius Peter Garesché was born near Havana, Cuba, in 1821. He graduated from West Point in 1841 and fought in the Mexican American War. In the fall of 1862, he was in uniform again, this time on the Union side in the US Civil War. On December 31, in the Battle of Stones River in Tennessee, he was killed by cannon fire. It was his first and last Civil War battle. Garesché was the highest-ranking Hispanic officer killed at Stones River.

Patrick Ronayne Cleburne

Cleburne was an Irish-born commander in the Confederate Army. He became known as the Stonewall Jackson of the West. Cleburne had a talent for fooling the enemy with his strategic plans. He also began the Confederate Army of the Freedmen. This army allowed enslaved people to enlist and buy their freedom.

Editor's note:
America is a nation of immigrants. This series celebrates important contributions immigrants have made to the military. In choosing the people to feature in this book, the author and 12-Story Library editors considered diversity of all kinds and the significance and stature of the work.

Glossary

blockade
An act of war that keeps people or supplies from entering or leaving a port or country. A blockade is usually done with ships.

cavalry
A military force mounted on horseback.

civilian
A person who is not in the military or police force. An ordinary citizen.

commission
To make someone an officer in the military.

composer
A person who writes music.

deploy
To send out troops for battle. To move as if being deployed.

GI Bill
A US law passed in 1944 giving benefits to veterans of World War II.

infantry
Soldiers who fight on foot.

jujitsu
A Japanese martial art where people fight without weapons.

mortarman
A soldier who operates a weapon called a mortar. A mortar is like a small canon.

NATO
An organization of countries in North America and Europe that have agreed to give each other military support. The letters stand for North Atlantic Treaty Organization.

quota
An official limit on something.

tuberculosis
An infectious disease caused by bacteria overgrowth usually affecting the lungs.

For More Information

Books

Baker, Bryann. *Life in America: Comparing Immigrant Experiences*, North Mankato, MN: Capstone Press, 2016.

Moss, Marrisa. *Nurse, Soldier, Spy: The Story of Sarah Edmonds, A Civil War Hero.* New York: Harry N. Abrams, 2011.

Wyckoff, Edwin Brit. *Helicopter Man: Igor Sikorsky and His Amazing Invention.* New York: Enslow Publishing, 2010.

Visit 12StoryLibrary.com

Scan the code or use your school's login at **12StoryLibrary.com** for recent updates about this topic and a full digital version of this book. Enjoy free access to:

- Digital ebook
- Breaking news updates
- Live content feeds
- Videos, interactive maps, and graphics
- Additional web resources

Note to educators: Visit 12StoryLibrary.com/register to sign up for free premium website access. Enjoy live content plus a full digital version of every 12-Story Library book you own for every student at your school.

Index

About the Author

Paige Smith is a writer in St. Paul, Minnesota. She is an avid reader and lover of art and history. Paige has a bachelor's degree in Communications, English, and Political Science from Ouachita University.